PASSIVE INCOME STEP-BY-STEP

Proven Guide to Start Making Money

Work From Home and Build Your Financial Freedom!

JONATHAN S. WALKER

Copyright © 2017 Jonathan S. Walker

All rights reserved.

DEDICATION

This Book Is Dedicated To All Who Desire To Be Financially Free. May Your Efforts Bear Fruits In the Near Future And I Wish You All The Success In Life.

&

I dedicate this book as well to my two beautiful children and my loving wife who have been nothing short of being my light and joy throughout the years.

CONTENTS

	Introduction	7
1	Chapter 1 – Surveys, Selling Photographs, And Teaching An Online Course	9
2	Chapter 2 – Passive Income Earned From Investing	16
3	Chapter 3- Start A Blog	22
4	Chapter 4 – Selling Products Online	27
5	Chapter 5 – Affiliate Marketing	31
6	Chapter 6 – Venture Capitalism	38
7	Conclusion	42

Copyright 2017 by Diana Watson - All rights reserved.

The following eBook is reproduced below with the goal of providing information that is as accurate and reliable as possible. Regardless, purchasing this eBook can be seen as consent to the fact that both the publisher and the author of this book are in no way experts on the topics discussed within and that any recommendations or suggestions that are made herein are for entertainment purposes only. Professionals should be consulted as needed prior to undertaking any of the action endorsed herein.

This declaration is deemed fair and valid by both the American Bar Association and the Committee of Publishers Association and is legally binding throughout the United States.

Furthermore, the transmission, duplication or reproduction of any of the following work including specific information will be considered an illegal act irrespective of if it is done electronically or in print. This extends to creating a secondary or tertiary copy of the work or a recorded copy and is only allowed with express written consent from the Publisher. All additional right reserved.

The information in the following pages is broadly considered to be a truthful and accurate account of facts and as such any inattention, use or misuse of the information in question by the reader will render any resulting actions solely under their purview. There are no scenarios in which the publisher or the original author of this work can be in any fashion deemed liable for any hardship or damages that may befall them after undertaking information described herein.

Additionally, the information in the following pages is intended only for informational purposes and should thus be thought of as universal. As befitting its nature, it is presented without assurance regarding its prolonged validity or interim quality. Trademarks that are mentioned are done without written consent and can in no way be considered an endorsement from the trademark holder.

INTRODUCTION

Before we get into the different types of passive income, let's first talk about what it actually is. Passive income is money that is earned from a source in which he or she is not physically involved. Like active income, passive income is taxed, though it is usually treated a little differently by the Internal Revenue Service (IRS). States differ slightly in their tax laws, so make sure to see a certified public accountant before filing your taxes with the IRS.

Overall, there are three types of income. Passive,

which is the subject of this e-book, active and portfolio income. To give a little insight into the difference between the three, we will briefly outline active and portfolio income before delving into different types of passive income.

Although it should seem self-explanatory, we are going to detail what active income is. Active income is a job that requires the earner to be physically present. In the United States, the most common forms of active income are hourly and salary. Hourly employees earn a wage for each hour they work while salary employees are paid a flat rate regardless of how many hours they put in. Most companies pay weekly or biweekly, although there are a few who pay monthly. However, those tend to be government or teaching positions.

Surprisingly enough, freelance work is also considered active income. The person in the freelance position gets paid for work upon its completion. One of the downfalls of freelance work is if you are sick or unable to complete a project, there is no paycheck. Writing articles, e-books and traditional books and photography are the most common types of freelance jobs.

Portfolio income is money earned from royalties, investments, capital gains and dividends. For tax purposes, the IRS does not consider portfolio income to be passive income as it does not come from traditional businesses or passive investments.

Now that we have talked about the different types of income let's talk about why passive income is a great way to earn extra money for savings, retirement, vacations or anything else you would like to spend your money on.

While you should be very excited about what we will learn in this book, it is important to note that passive income does not mean 'easy money.' Like all other forms of income, there is some work involved whether it is research, development, writing an e-book or selling photographs online. Wouldn't turning a hobby into income be an excellent way to earn some extra money? One of the ways we will discuss in this book is exactly that. Even using a hobby to earn a passive income takes some time and effort up front, although it is probably the most enjoyable of all the forms of passive income, we will cover in this book.

If you have some time and energy to devote to passive income from the comfort of your own home (maybe even in your pajamas while you sip coffee), let's talk about some of the exciting ways you can earn a passive income!

Chapter 1

Surveys, Selling Photos

& Teaching Classes

Surprisingly enough, there are lots of ways to make money on the internet. We will list some of the more passive ways to earn money online and then give you some insight into how you can get going with passive income online.

Websites like InboxDollars actually pay people to shop online, play games and even search the web. InboxDollars has been around since 2000, and the company itself employs thirty people. They offer anywhere between 1-10 cents per email read and the payment on playing games or going to an affiliate website varies. As with any web-based income potential, there are pros and cons to InboxDollars. The first payment isn't sent until you've earned thirty bucks. At that, it can take up to two weeks to receive payment so if you are looking for quick and easy, InboxDollars isn't the place to be. However, if you are hanging out in front of a computer while sipping on a latte at your local coffee shop, why not sign up and earn some money simply for surfing the net or reading emails? You are already online anyway, right?

Another site similar to InboxDollars is called **SwagBucks.** InboxDollars website is a little easier to maneuver, and they categorize each option for earning cash online. SwagBucks does require you to sign up with them before you can see the earning potential. Swagbucks doesn't pay in cold, hard cash. They pay in the form of "SwagBucks," which is their term for earning points. Each SwagBuck is approximately one cent. That means once you've accrued one-hundred, you've made roughly one dollar. SwagBucks are redeemable for gift cards only. There are no checks or payments sent to your PayPal account. As opposed to InboxDollars, SwagBucks will actually pay you for referrals, in the form of their SwagBucks, of course. For every survey your referral completes, you get ten percent. That's actually a great deal considering it is someone else doing the work, right? One last thing to mention about these websites. They both pay you to sign up for trial offers, which is something you need to be very careful with. While they both will pay a pretty decent amount for your signing up, you have to remember to cancel your membership within the month, or your credit card will be charged for the service. Of the two, Swagbucks pays more; usually enough to earn a twenty-five dollar gift card, which is actually a fantastic deal!

In addition to earning a passive income by signing up for websites like those mentioned previously, you can also sell your photography online. Obviously, this is geared toward those who enjoy taking photos as a hobby. As it isn't for everyone, we will discuss it briefly before moving onto the next subject.

If you do enjoy taking photos of scenic overlooks, nature, or even people (with their permission of course), you can sell your photos to places like Shutterstock and

Stock photo. Depending on which site you choose, they will pay either with a percentage of overall sales of your photo or a flat fee for each photo that is sold to the client. One of the great things about selling your photos is one picture can earn money more than once. Each time it is sold, you'll get a percentage (or the aforementioned flat fee). If you always liked photography but hadn't really given it a second thought, maybe now is the time to do so. You do have to go out and take the pictures, but it is a great way to get some exercise, fresh air, see some awesome sights and earning some of that passive income!

Another way to earn passive income is to write an e-book. Like photography, it has to be something that you have an interest in. Since it isn't everyone's cup of tea, we'll go over it briefly, just like we did with photography.

There are several ways to make money with writing e-books. Fiction, fantasy, how-to, cookbooks...the list is endless. There is some work up front, and if you aren't the best with commas and periods, it might be prudent to hire an editor just to make sure you don't miss anything major. Some of the most popular books are how to and fantasy. If you are particularly knowledgeable on a subject, or you have an incredibly active imagination, either of those would be an excellent way to start earning passive income.

Once the book is written, you can publish it on Amazon and wait for some money to start coming in. If you want to make decent money, you will want to invest some time in marketing. This is something you can do yourself using your already established social media outlets. Facebook, Twitter, and Instagram are great for free advertising.

Did you know that you can make money by posting YouTube videos online? This too takes some work and a bit of marketing on your part, but once you get going who knows? Maybe you will be the next YouTube sensation! As we outlined with writing an e-book, there are several areas in which you can create a YouTube channel. Book or restaurant reviews, music, opinions, comedy, music and tutorials of all kinds including hair, makeup, rebuilding engines or fixing just about anything around the house. From sinks to refrigerators, people are always looking for a way to fix things themselves so that they don't have to spend thousands of dollars hiring someone to come out to their house and take care of it for them. The key to success with this type of internet income is marketing. We already talked about those social media outlets in the e-book section. You can utilize those to market your YouTube videos as well. Making the video itself is not as easy as it sounds, but it can be quite a bit of fun. There will be some trial and error, and once it's done there will be some editing involved, but it is free to post videos to YouTube meaning no upfront cost. You'll only need to put the time and energy into creating your YouTube masterpiece.

The last topic we'll go over for internet income is creating an online course or an online guide. Is there something that you are particularly great at? Perhaps you know a lot about medieval history, how to rebuild a transmission for a particular or rare car, or maybe you can teach people how to sell real estate. Really, whatever you are good at and/or passionate about, you can create a course to help others who might be looking to expand their own knowledge base.

While there are a few platforms in which you can do this, one of the best-known platforms is Udemy.com. They have over *eight million* students looking to learn something new every day. That is a huge number of people to whom you can sell your product. What's great about this is there isn't a whole lot you need to do in the way of marketing. Udemy has it all categorized. You would want to write a killer description of your tutorial, though. That way, you would have a bit of an advantage over others who might be teaching related online courses. This is literally something you can make money at while you sleep. Your course can include a video, tutorials, lessons and checklists. What's great about Udemy is you can make it your own. There are even several price points for this website meaning you can have a higher price point that has all the bells and whistles and then lower price points that have a little less, but still the same great information you are providing at the higher price. This makes it so you can market to a larger group of people maximizing your potential for passive income.

Finally, you can make an online guide. Again, the possibilities here are endless. You can create a guide to the best fishing in the country, white water rafting, skiing...whatever you'd like. Online guides don't usually cost anything to the person searching for those items. Where you make your money with guides is through advertisers. If you are creating a guide to fishing, you'd want to check with bait shops and any outdoorsy type retail place that would want to place an ad on your site. Some pay by the click, others pay if someone purchases something through their website after clicking from your guide. It depends on the retailer, but this is a great way to earn passive income. What's not to love about sharing your expertise and making money in the process?

We've covered quite a few things in this opening chapter! We have outlined just a few of the ways you can earn a passive income using the internet. One of the best things about the things we talked about is they can be fun, especially if writing or photography is a hobby. Taking surveys probably isn't how you picture yourself spending your weekend, but when it comes to passive income, you have to admit that clicking through a survey or getting paid to play a new online game is pretty passive. That being said, there are much more ways and exploring those is just a Google search away. Find something that interests you and the sky is the limit.

Chapter 2 – Passive Income Earned From Investing

Investing may sound daunting. It's highly likely you are looking to passive income as a way to make money because you don't have a lot of excess cash laying around. Let's face it...the majority of us don't. While investing may sound intimidating and expensive, rest assured there are ways to earn a passive income without having to put a second mortgage on your house or dip into your children's college funds.

One of the first things you can look at in the way of investing is joining a Lending Club. This is a web-based lending program geared toward peer to peer borrowing and lending. Unlike traditional investing in US Treasury

Securities or bank certificates, Lending Clubs offer a much higher yield on returns. Bonds and other bank certificates usually earn about one-percent which is passive income in the basest of terms. Making that little every year won't do much in the way of helping you retire sooner or get to that beach house you've been looking to vacation at for the past few years. Lending Clubs have a much higher interest rate and with that comes an increased risk. Like bank loans, those given through a Lending Club are at risk of default meaning if the borrower doesn't repay the note to you, that's money you've just lost on investment.

The risk of a defaulted loan is minimal if you know what kinds of loans are more likely to be paid back. For example, you wouldn't want to invest in a mom and pop coffee shop that is slotted for location in the midst of several big chain coffee shops. While that is a risk that can pay off, it might be a little too risky for your liking. And that's okay! When it comes to investing, you have to do what makes you comfortable. Especially when we are talking about putting up some of your own, hard-earned money. Remember, the thought of doing that might make you a little uneasy, but the payoff can be very rewarding.

Lending Clubs usually recommend you start out with an initial deposit of around 2500.00. You can invest as little as twenty-five dollars on a single loan, meaning you can actually invest in up to one-hundred businesses at a time. The potential for earning passive income using this method is higher, and you are invested in businesses that you didn't have to put all your blood, sweat and tears into starting up. That's pretty passive and far less stressful. The beautiful thing about Lending Clubs is there are several that are free to join. That's great if you know a good chunk of what you do have saved is going to go to the initial deposit.

In terms of investing, you can also look into Index Funds. It is a form of mutual fund that helps you to invest in the stock market in an entirely passive manner. These is especially great because you don't have to concern yourself with choosing an investment, knowing when to buy or sell, or rebalancing your portfolio. All of those things are handled by the index fund.

One of the best sites to set up an index fund is Scottrade. Their website is easy to maneuver, setting up an account is pretty affordable. Their website offers levels of investment and depending on how much you invest; you'll also be rewarded with a minimum of fifty free trades. It's a pretty awesome deal. Not to mention, you get to choose where your money goes. Also, if you set up with Scottrade and decide to invest in a different manner, you'll already have an account established with them. Along the same lines as investing, if you are looking to get a retirement fund going (outside of a traditional 401k you may have through your full-time job), Roth IRA's are a great place to put your money. And, if you leave your job you can roll your 401k into a Roth IRA without having to pay huge tax penalties.

Another way to invest online is the use of a Robo-advisor. If you are worried about trying to decipher stocks and how the market works, let a Robo-advisor do the job for you. One Robo-advisor that gets some of the best reviews is Betterment. You provide them with the funds, and their algorithms will find the best investments for you. In addition to that, it will keep your portfolio balanced. Talk about passive! While there is the upfront cost of investing, you won't have to stress over reading the paper or watching the news every day to see where your stocks are at.

One of the most well-known and popular ways of investing is in the Real Estate Market. As with most investments, this can come with some risk, and there are more ways to invest in Real Estate than just flipping houses or turning them into rental properties. Because rental properties are the most common, we will discuss them in a little greater detail.

Real Estate rentals aren't entirely passive income makers. There is some work involved in finding the house or apartment complex, but once you've found a property and rented it out, you'll only need to make sure your tenant sends you a rent check every month. You can also hire property management companies to manage your rental for you. Their typical fee is approximately ten-percent of the rental amount every month. One of the benefits of rental properties is once the original loan is paid off, your earnings go up substantially. If you have more than one property that's paid off and bringing in decent rent each month, you might even be able to retire and turn your investments into full-fledged passive income.

Along the same lines, you can also invest in Real Estate Investment Trusts, also known as REITs. As previously mentioned, investing in real estate itself isn't entirely passive. However, if you want to invest in real estate completely passively, REITs are the way to go. This is kind of like investing in a mutual fund with various real estate projects as opposed to stocks or bonds. Like mutual funds, REITs are managed by professionals, so you won't have to worry about learning all the legalities of real estate. REITs pay a higher dividend than most bonds, stocks or even bank investments. You can also sell your REIT at any time making it a more fluid form of passive income since you'll never actually have to invest in an actual property.

There is one final note we'll mention in regards to real estate. If you already own your own home and have some space available, you can rent out that unused space on Airbnb. It's a relatively new concept, but over the past year, it has exploded all around the globe. This engine allows people to travel all over the world and stay places much cheaper than hotels, hostels or traditional bed and breakfasts. By signing up for Airbnb, you can earn money simply by renting out your unused space to travelers. Obviously, there is some risk involved, but Airbnb has a community safety and standards expectations for people renting their space as well as those seeking places to stay. A form of government-issued identification is required so there isn't much to worry about in the way of hosting a felon. The site provides income examples, and a relatively easy search showed that one room in Denver, Colorado can go for as much as 250.00 per week. Not bad for passive income and the best part about this is, you already *own* the investment property.

Chapter 3 – Start a Blog

There are many things you can do with a blog, but we'll focus on two. Creating your own and buying an existing blog. Creating your own won't be entirely passive, but once again, it is easier than finding a part-time job. And with most passive income internet based ventures, you can do this from the comfort of your couch. You aren't going to miss out on cherished family time or dinner because you had to go from your full-time job to the part-time job.

The trick to blogging is consistency. Thousands of blogs are created every year, and the majority of them are abandoned within a few months. Blogging is a competitive market and if it is something you choose to do, remember to stay consistent, post on a regular basis, market using other social media sites we've discussed previously. Passive income from blogging comes mostly from advertisements. Those big-time advertisers are looking for blogs that get a lot of traffic to advertise their product. This will require some work at the beginning with posting, marketing and reaching out to advertisers to get them to pay you to advertise on your blog. If you like to write, or you have an idea for something that's funny tech savvy, or just completely different, blogging is a great way to earn that semi-passive income.

To be clear, one can't expect to make decent passive income by writing and publishing any old blog. In my quest to find what people are most interested in reading about, I came across a list of a whopping *eighty-one* ideas for writing a blog that will sell. We won't be covering all, but I'm going to list the top ten.

1. **Self-improvement and Self-hypnosis**. Whether you go into a bookstore or are looking for books online, self-improvement is one that piques a lot of people's interest. No one is perfect, and most people are looking for a way to improve themselves. Whether it'd be through physical fitness or having a more positive attitude in life, there are literally hundreds, if not thousands of self-improvement topics to blog about. Self-hypnosis is incredibly interesting. It isn't what you think, either. We've all seen the silly reality shows

where people using hypnosis make their subjects act out of sorts. Self-hypnosis in this context actually goes hand in hand with self-improvement. Self-hypnosis is about meditating your way to a different you. Whether you need to boost your self-esteem or work on confidence and overall outlook on life, self-hypnosis is something that people are highly interested in.

2. **Health and Fitness for Busy People**. This is kind of along the same lines as self-improvement. Many people want to get in better shape, but who really has the time? A blog about fitness for people who are always on the go (and not working on earning passive incomes like we are) would be a great target audience. Plus, many sports and activity retailers would love to pay to advertise on a site that is suggesting people get into shape. Everything they need to attain their goals is a click away...from *your* blog.

3. **Language and Learning Blogs.** These can be lumped in with creating that online course we discussed earlier. As a matter of fact, should you choose to teach a course, you could include blogs from your personal site as part of the learner's course and content. The language might be a little more difficult if you are only fluent in one, but learning new things always appeals to people.

4. **Earning extra money.** Who better to write a blog about this subject than you? You're well on your way to earning passive income without having to get a second job, right? There are quite a few blogs that discuss passive income, but there aren't many that detail trials, tribulations, and successes. It'd be a nice little niche for you to slide right into.

5. **Food blogs.** We aren't talking about the local pub or fast food chain. Specialty or unique/rare foods are what interests people. "Foodie" blogs come and go, but the same applies here as it did with fitness. Rating food and restaurants in a way that

gets people to read your blog over others will entice advertisers to pay for space on your blog. And, you get to go out and try all kinds of amazing new foods. Sounds like a win-win situation.

So, we've talked about creating your own blog, but what if you aren't interested in writing them yourself? Perhaps you don't quite have the time to invest in doing some research and writing the blog, then finding advertisers for your site. That's okay; there is another way to earn a passive income by purchasing a pre-existing blog. The interesting thing about this idea is all the content is there. You will have to put some effort into maintaining the site, but all the bare bones are set up for you.

A lot of blogs use Google AdSense, which is what provides a monthly income for a blogger. It is based on the ads Google places on their site or blog. Blogs tend to sell for approximately twenty-four times their average monthly income. For instance, if a blog earns two-hundred and fifty dollars per month, the most you'll pay for that blog is three-thousand dollars. Like we mentioned in the chapter about investing in real estate, some things will require a bit of money up front. If you are able to afford this route with buying a blog, keep in mind that if the site is generating two-fifty per month, you will earn your money back in a year. After that, the blog will be making money that will be all profit. With a little effort put into the blog to make sure content remains up to date, it'll be mostly passive and something you can do in your spare time.

Chapter 4 – Selling Products Online

There are a couple of ways to make money by selling products online to earn a passive income. Actually, there are several, but the point of this book is passive income, so we will stick to discussing two great ways to make that money using a website. Drop ship products for another retailer, or sell your own products online. If you don't want to invest a lot of money in products to stock your online store, drop shipping might be more appealing. In this chapter, we will cover both so you can get a good idea as to what will work best for you and fit into your budget.

Drop shipping isn't entirely passive, but it's one of the closest things you can to do earn that passive income. What is it, you ask? Drop shipping is where a product goes directly from the manufacturer to the customer.

And, where do you fit into this equation? You would be the middle man. Drop shipping requires a little effort in that you'd need to set up a website to sell a product. What's particularly significant about this is, you don't have to spend the time creating a product, then marketing it online, calculating sales, paying people to help you out...none of that. The middle man in this scenario simply has the product on their site, and when people arrive to purchase, the order is either automatically or manually forwarded to the manufacturer. The product is then "drop shipped" to the customer. This means you will never have to get your hands dirty. The passive income part of this scenario comes from your earning a percentage of the sales of whatever product or products you have on your website.

In addition to simply being the middle man, let's talk about some other benefits to using drop shipping as your passive income source. One of the biggest advantages is that the startup for this is minuscule, especially compared to some of the other things we've mentioned such as real estate and purchasing a blog. You will also be able to offer an extensive selection and wide variety of products without ever having to purchase the product, store it, then pay to have it shipped to the customer.

The risk is reduced tremendously with drop shipping. Most retailers who set up a website and sell the product have to invest hundreds or even thousands of dollars up front to build their inventory. Drop shipping requires you purchase the product only briefly, then have it shipped directly to the customer. The upfront cost of drop shipping is pretty minimal. You also don't need to worry about renting space to house the product. The store you own is virtual which means you can run your drop ship business from the comfort of your own home. Or, anywhere that has wifi.

What's important to mention about drop shipping is if you want to be successful, you'll need to find a specialized niche. In order to do well with drop shipping, you'll want to do a little research and find retailers that utilize that service. Don't narrow yourself to one or two markets. In the beginning, start small, but the more you are able to expand and the more products you are able to add to your website, the more likely you are to earn a pretty decent passive income.

When it comes to selling your own products on the internet, the possibilities are endless. Online, you can sell any service or product that you can think of. It could be anything from a product you've created, things of a digital nature like software or DVDs, even instructional videos if you have them. If not, this is a great opportunity for you to create them, as discussed in the section regarding Udemy or YouTube videos.

If you don't have want to setup your own website, you can work with affiliates who are willing to sell your product for you. In this instance, it would be like your partner is the drop shipper or middle man and you are the retailer. Either way is perfectly acceptable and a great way to earn a passive income.

How much money you make depends on how much time you are willing to commit to this venture. One story that is particularly intriguing is that of a woman who was able to quit her job and earn one-hundred thousand dollars a year with her online store. Now, let's be clear that this isn't the norm. The reason she was able to make so much money was that she'd found that special niche. Her online store specializes in making handkerchiefs for special occasions like weddings. They don't just produce handkerchiefs, though. They make linen party favor bags, lace umbrellas, pillowcases and much more. That is the kind of idea that will earn significant money. Get those wheels in your head spinning! Undoubtedly you've had some magnificent ideas for products that are unique or even those that would simplify your daily life.

Along these lines, you can also set up a website to sell products that you are familiar with. This is similar to selling your own product except you don't have to create a product...you'll be selling someone else's product. With this concept, you could start out small with one or two products, and after a while, you can add other products that are closely related to what you've already begun to sell. You'd want to make the products similar to avoid needing a large website to sell hundreds of products.

Keeping your site neat, clean and straightforward will bring more traffic.

Chapter 5 – Affiliate Marketing

When it comes to passive income, the majority of people who get into it start out in affiliate marketing. While the concept has been around for quite some time, it became popular after the 4-Hour Work Week was released. Ever since then, people have been excited to find a way to "make money while they sleep." The idea behind affiliate marketing is you earn a commission by promoting other people's products. You make money when a sale is completed thanks to your marketing. This relies heavily on revenue sharing, which can go either way. That means that if you have a product and are looking to sell more of it, you can offer promoters financial incentive for marketing your product. Alternatively, if you do not have a product of your own, you can still make money by promoting a product you believe in or are familiar with.

In this chapter, we are going to get into detail as to

what affiliate marketing is and how you can get started earning passive income by using it.

Conversely, there are three or four sides to affiliate marketing, depending on which definition you are looking at. For all intents and purposes, when it comes down to it, there are really only two sides to this marketing equation. There are the product seller and creator on the one hand and the marketer on the other. In affiliate marketing, you can be both the creator and the marketer and profit from 'shared' revenue.

Let's take a closer look at all the working parts of what makes affiliate marketing such a successful venture.

There is the merchant, who can also be the creator, seller, retailer, brand or vendor. Ultimately, the merchant is the creator of the product. For example, Dyson vacuum cleaners. On a smaller scale, it can be a person who creates and sells online courses to people wishing to further their education without having to go back to college. From the solo entrepreneur to online startup companies and even Fortune 500 companies, just about anyone can be the merchant who is behind the affiliate marketing system. The merchant doesn't have to be actively involved. They only have to be able to offer a product to sell.

The next party is the affiliate who is also sometimes referred to as the publisher. Like the merchant, the affiliate can be an entire company or an individual. The affiliate is where the marketing happens. They are the party responsible for promoting one or several products in an attempt to attract and even convince those potential customers that the product is needed or of great value and the customer winds up purchasing this product because of the marketing. One way this type of marketing is achieved is by a review of the product being sold with a blog. Really, this can be done on any social media outlet and Facebook is getting to be a huge platform for affiliate marketing. Perhaps you hadn't noticed it before, but you likely will now. Maybe one of your friends posted something about a product they liked. If you went to that website and bought a product, your friend might have been compensated and would be the affiliate.

Now, while there are two parties to the actual functionality of affiliate marketing, there is one key component to recognize, and that is the customer. Without people to consume the product, there would be no need for affiliate marketing, right?

The consumer or customer might be unaware that they are involved in affiliate marketing. That depends on how the affiliate markets the product. Some affiliates let their customers know up front that they are trying to sell a particular product. Others are more passive in using ads or links in their blogs for people to follow to certain websites. No matter how the consumer gets to the product, the affiliate is paid a commission if there is a sale, so long as there is an agreement between the affiliate and the merchant. Nine times out of ten, there is some sort of arrangement between the two parties. Most people don't tend to push a product without having an incentive to do so. Whether the affiliate gets paid in free product or cold hard cash is something to be worked out between the marketer and affiliate. If you choose to be an affiliate for a product to earn passive income, make sure your contract is clear so that no matter which form of payment is received, you will actually be compensated for your time and effort in marketing the product.

At the beginning of this chapter, we talked about three to four components to affiliate marketing. Because most people only see three true components, we will not go into too much detail with the fourth. However, it should be mentioned, albeit briefly.

The fourth component is the network. In most cases, the network acts as an intermediary between the merchant and the affiliate. The network tends to handle payment between the merchant and the affiliate. They can also be responsible for shipping and delivery of the product being sold. The use of a network is not required, although some bigger corporations tend to use the networks to promote, ship and deliver their product. A good example of a network is Amazon. That website sells everything you can think of from tools and books to toys and household items. They have an Amazon Associate program that allows you to promote any item you sell on their platform. Of course, Amazon charges a fee for this, though it is usually pretty minimal.

Now, there are four simple steps to becoming either a merchant or an affiliate. Most people begin with affiliate because it is slightly easier than starting out as a merchant. We will provide you with the four steps for each so that you can make an informed decision as to which route you'd prefer to take to start earning your passive income.

Becoming an Online Merchant in 4 steps:

1. You need to have an idea for a product. This is tough because many people have it in their head that coming up with an idea is hard, which isn't necessarily true. What happens with most people is they have an idea that they are in love with and that is where the problem is. They become too focused on that *one* idea. To get started as a

merchant, you'll want to find products out there that are already selling well, but that the market isn't already flooded with. You need something that people will want to buy and will be able to use on a daily basis. Perhaps you have an idea that will make household chores easier or a product that can clean as well as bleach without all the toxic fumes. Take a little bit of time and do some research on Google to find ideas or products you can get behind.

2. The second step is to validate your idea. You wouldn't want to make or back a product without knowing that there would be reasonable interest for people to purchase it. Ask family, friends, work associates...anyone you know will be *honest* with you about the product you are looking to sell. Sometimes, that can be tough with family and friends because they want to support you in your ventures. Make sure you are asking people you know will tell you the absolute truth.

3. Create your product or prepare to market the already established product you've decided to sell. Creating products can be costly up front. However, if you've done research, had plenty of people tell you they'd definitely buy it and you are passionate about it, go for it!

4. Finally, once your product is ready, you'll need to find the affiliates willing to sell and market your product on your behalf.

Becoming an Online Affiliate in 4 steps:

1. First and foremost, start reviewing the products in your chosen niche. You can do this via YouTube, a blog or live streams on a platform like Periscope.

2. Collect emails so that you can connect with your audience.

3. Check out joint venture webinars. It is a great platform to make a lot of sales in a shorter period of time. At the same time, you'll be growing your email list and expanding your customer base.

4. Finally, once you get your affiliate business to a point where it is making money you can scale growth by using pay per click advertising.

To recap, there are two ways to get into affiliate marketing; becoming an affiliate or becoming a merchant. With what we've outlined here today, I'm positive you'll be able to find which route works best for you. Perhaps you'll discover you can do both!

Chapter 6 – Venture Capitalism

Investopedia defines venture capitalism as a person who provides capital for startup ventures or one who supports small companies that want to expand but lack access to equities markets. Venture capitalists are people who are willing to invest in these companies because they know they will earn significant returns on the companies if they are successful. There is some risk in investing in companies that are in the startup phase because most new businesses fail within the first year. If it is a risk you are financially able to take, it's an easy way to earn a passive income. The venture capitalist provides the money up front, and when the business succeeds, they get to sit back and relax while the money rolls in.

While there are several paths to becoming a venture capitalist, there are two that are most common and, quite frankly, the simplest to get into. Serial entrepreneurship and tech-oriented investment banking.

The serial entrepreneur differs from a typical entrepreneur in that they will come up with an idea for business, get it started, and then hand the reigns over to someone else. An entrepreneur that is not serial will start a business, get it through the first year and beyond and stick with it until they retire or sell the business. Typically, they do not start more than one business whereas a serial entrepreneur will do this several times throughout their business life. This is ideal for people who have lots of great ideas and want to share them with the world. Once the business is up and running, the serial entrepreneur will earn a passive income from all the businesses they get started. Like many forms of passive income and as we've mentioned a time or two, getting on the road to passive income will take some work. Ultimately, when you are earning money without having to leave your home, whatever you put into the idea, in the beginning, will clearly be worth it.

In addition to the ability to spot a great investment from a mile away, a serial entrepreneur is also great at motivating people and inspiring others to follow them. They are willing to take a personal and business risk. They have the ability to recognize a great market to invest in consistently. Some people have made their career being a serial entrepreneur. Realistically, you could help several businesses get their start, which would not be passive. However, once those businesses are up, running and making good money, all you have to do is sit back and enjoy the fruits of your labor. And that, my friend, is the definition of passive income.

The second is the tech-oriented investment banker. Of the two, this is becoming less common because the risk associated is higher. An investment banker, in general, is someone who provides the capital for business...any business. Now, as we have mentioned previously, for this section, we are specifically talking about tech-oriented investments. These tend to be a little less risky because of the way technology is evolving. People are always looking for the next new, really impressive technological advancement. For this type of venture capitalism, you would invest in some kind of emerging technology, and when it succeeds, you will get to reap the rewards of getting in on this investment on the ground floor. As we have talked about previously, finding a specific niche or even an area of technology in which you are particularly well versed is a great way to keep your risk a little lower. That being said, you probably would not want to invest in several tech companies right away. The point of passive income is earned money with less stress than having to go out and find a part-time job. Do a little research on emerging technologies and find the one you are most confident in.

As we've gone over a few times so far, any kind of investing comes with risk. Of the two most common forms of investing through venture capitalism, you are more likely to succeed and experience less risk with serial entrepreneurship. That being said, if you are very tech savvy and can recognize a great product easily, go that route. Remember, you are trying to get yourself to a point where you are earning that passive income, and that means finding exactly what is going to work best for you.

Conclusion

The topics we covered are just a few of the most popular and more importantly, they are proven to be the most successful ways of making money passively. Whether you prefer to earn a passive income by selling photos or e-books or you are the type to get out and become a venture capitalist, what you need to remember is to keep your goal in the forefront of your mind. There will be trials and tribulations no matter what you choose. Stay focused, keep positive and you can most certainly find the niche that best fits your lifestyle.

I hope this book was able to help you to find a way to earn a passive income successfully and without having to go out and find a part-time job.

The next step is to test out a few of the tips and tricks to find the ones you like most for the type of passive income that will work best for you. The key component is to really take some time to consider where your passion lies because earning a passive income is about doing something you enjoy while making money passively... possibly even while you sleep!

THANK YOU

Dear treasured reader, I would like to thank you from the bottom of my heart purchasing this valuable resource on building a passive income. I sincerely hope the book is able to help you realize your dream of being financially free by giving you several choices and strategies for building profitable online ventures.

I hope you've gotten some valuable information that you can use daily to better your life and those around you as well. If you liked it would you be so kind as to leave an honest/positive review for my book. I would appreciate it very much.

Here's to your financially free, rewarding and profitable life.

To Your Success,

Jonathan S. Walker

www.ingramcontent.com/pod-product-compliance
Lightning Source LLC
LaVergne TN
LVHW010435070526
838199LV00066B/6037